CONTENTS

GET HAPPY OR DIE TRYING

How to Bounce Back, Come Up, and Thrive Straight Outta of Chaos

Will G Woodard

WGW Publishing

COPYRIGHT

Get Happy or Die Trying: How to Bounce Back, Come Up, and Thrive Straight Outta of Chaos

Disclaimer

The information presented in this book is for informational and inspirational purposes only. It is not intended as a substitute for professional medical, psychological, or psychiatric advice, diagnosis, or treatment. The author is not a licensed therapist, doctor, or mental health professional, and the content provided here is based on personal experiences, insights, and research.

Readers are encouraged to consult with a qualified healthcare provider or mental health professional for any concerns regarding their physical, mental, or emotional well-being. Any reliance on the information in this book is at the reader's own discretion. The author and publisher assume no responsibility for actions taken by readers as a result of the content in this book.

Remember, self-help is an ongoing journey, and professional guidance can be a valuable part of that process.

First Edition - November 2024

For my wife Joy; my late mother, Dora; my children, and those who refuse to let life's adversities define them.

Preface

Note from the Author

To be real, this book is a journey of resilience, growth, and self-discovery—a journey I've traveled while facing some harsh trials, including several years in federal prison. These pages hold the insights I've gained from experiences rooted in some pretty dark places. Here's the deal: life's toughest experiences often become our greatest teachers. They shape us, and stretch us, and if we let them transform us in unexpected ways. Now, let's keep it real—the lessons I'm sharing here are uniquely mine, but the bigger ideas about resilience, shifting perspectives, and finding strength in the chaos are not at all new.

Some forward thinkers have been saying these things for years—people like Viktor Frankl, who taught about finding meaning in darkness (Man's Search for Meaning); Ryan Holiday, who shows how setbacks are often setups for comebacks (The Obstacle is the Way); and Brené Brown, who's brought vulnerability and self-compassion to the forefront (The Gifts of Imperfection). Their work helped me and so many others find courage in being real. To keep it real—I couldn't have figured this all out on my own. I'm grateful for the ways they helped me set my path. We will touch on these insights moving ahead.

Here's some truth about happiness most of us know, but barely ever think about: happiness is fragile, unpredictable, circumstantial and sometimes feels out of reach. One minute you have it, and the next, it slips from your grasp. But here's what I've learned—happiness isn't a "once and done" deal. Sometimes life hits hard, things change, and happiness becomes this constant game of ups and downs. It’s a journey we have to keep choosing, over and over. Here’s the deal: what truly matters is the determination to stay in the game, to keep pursuing happiness. Life “feels” better being happy or experiencing the energy of moving toward it–just keep moving.

Introduction

From Million-Dollar Deal Maker to Prison Inmate-Mentor

Here's the Deal: Life knocked me flat and turned everything upside down. Back in 2014, I found myself up against a U.S. federal prosecutor deadset on getting me convicted in a multimillion-dollar fraud case. The Feds wanted a fast conviction, offering me an out. A five-year plea deal that would've shaved time off what potentially could be an eighteen-year prison sentence, if convicted at trial. But keeping it real: I couldn't take the deal. I wasn't about to plead guilty to something that exaggerated my actions or intentions, and I wasn't going to let a court-appointed attorney, someone who wasn't fully committed to my defense speak for me. I fired two court-appointed attorneys.

Though afraid, I decided to fight back, taking my case into my own hands, representing myself in two trials. The first trial was a wild ride that ended in a hung jury. But the second… It was like stepping into the ring against two determined tag-team opponents. This time I faced a man and a woman prosecutor while key witnesses for my defense took the Fifth, one after another, shattering critical parts of my defense. With the odds significantly stacked against me, I was convicted and handed a seven-year sentence in federal prison. It was a devastating knockdown blow. But that day, as the gavel came down, I had to make a choice. Let the conviction and sentence define me and be a knockout blow, or I decide right then and there to bounce back, despite how hard I'd fallen.

Prison didn't just take my freedom; it stripped away the life I knew. I was angry—at the system, at those witnesses who wouldn't stand up for me, and even angry at God. But here's what's up: staying angry wasn't going to help me; it would only keep me down. So, I decided to turn that anger into positive energy and purpose. I found myself sharing my faith, and mentoring younger inmates who were in some dark places, some who were contemplating taking their own lives. I realized that helping these guys wasn't just a lifeline for them—it was one for me, too. Nudged by a fellow inmate, I took up writing–and learned to write books and screenplays, turning the story of my pain into purpose, page by page.

I also studied law, wrote several petitions to overturn my conviction, and wrote sentencing reconsideration petitions for other inmates—some were successful, but not for me. The strength and insight I gained in those tough, dark places, that's what I want to share with you here. This book isn't about putting a positive spin on life's hardest moments or pretending that unfair situations are easy to “get over.” It’s about finding the grit to create your happiness, no matter what’s been stacked against you or how hard you’ve been hit. Here’s the deal: life will throw knockdown punches. But deciding if and how you bounce back, and come up again, is all on you. So let’s dive in. Let’s get into what it takes to turn life’s hardest hits into a comeback story that’s yours to write—and is the story you deserve.

Table of Contents

Chapter 2: The Power of Perspective:

Seeing Things Differently to Tackle Life's Problems

Chapter 3: Facing the Fall:

Handling Setbacks Head-On Without Fear

Chapter 4: Rising from the Ashes:

Starting Over and Finding New Purpose

Chapter 5: Reclaiming Your Power:

Taking Back Control of Your Life

Chapter 6: Finding Purpose in the Process:
Discovering Meaning in Every Step You Take

Chapter 7: The Strength in Vulnerability:

Finding True Strength by Being Open

Chapter 8: Building Your Resilience Toolbox:

Gearing Up with Tools for Tough Times

Chapter 9: The Power of Patience:

Learning to Stay Calm While You Wait

Chapter 10: Building Inner Strength:

Developing Unshakable Confidence from Within

Chapter 11: Finding Purpose in the Pain:
Turning Hard Times into Personal Growth

Chapter 19: Cultivating Inner Peace:

Finding Calm in Chaotic Surroundings

Chapter 20: Finding Peace Through Meditation:

Getting Clear and Calm from the Inside Out

Chapter 21: Tuning into Brain Frequencies:

Supercharging Your Mind to Boost Calm, Courage, and Confidence

Chapter 22: Happiness: Your Secret to Staying Young, Mind, Body, and Spirit

I write this book, dedicated to my family and readers who want to live in a happy space and are determined to get there, no matter the obstacles.

CHAPTER 1: WHAT IS YOUR PRISON?

Identifying and Breaking Free from What's Holding You Back

When we think of prison, towering walls and iron bars might come to mind, but that's just one kind of prison. The truth is, we all face different types of prisons in our lives—some are physical, but many are invisible, crafted by our own choices and circumstances. Here's what's up: understanding and naming these personal prisons is the first step toward gaining true freedom.

Identifying Your Prisons Prisons can come in many forms. It could be a job that drains your spirit, a toxic relationship that you can't seem to escape, or even a mindset that keeps you from moving forward. For some, it's the tangible bars of a cell, but for many, it's something much less visible. Let's keep it real: recognizing these prisons is crucial because you can't break free from what you don't acknowledge.

1. Job Prison: You spend your days watching the clock, feeling undervalued and overworked. It's not just about hating your job; it's about feeling trapped in a cycle that seems impossible to escape.

2. Relationship Prison: Whether with a friend, family member, or partner, these are relationships that bring more pain than joy. They hold you back rather than lift you up.

3. Self-Made Prison: This might be the hardest to face. It's built from our fears, insecurities, and negative self-talk. It's the inner voice that says, "You can't," when you should be saying, "I will."

Deciding to Be Free Acknowledging your personal prisons is only the beginning. Deciding to be free means making tough choices and sometimes enduring even tougher changes. Here's the deal: freedom requires action. It's not about one grand gesture, but rather a series of decisions that collectively lead to a larger change.

Planning Your Prison Break Every prison has a weakness, a way out. It starts with setting clear goals and understanding what freedom looks like for you. It could be finding a new job, ending a harmful relationship, or challenging your self-limiting beliefs.

Exercise for the Reader: Knowing Your Prison and Getting Free 1. List Your Prisons: Take a moment to write down the areas of your life where you feel stuck or constrained. Be honest and specific.

2. **Freedom Goals:** For each 'prison' you've listed, write down one realistic goal that moves you towards freedom. These should be tangible and measurable.

3. **Small Steps:** Break down each goal into smaller, actionable steps. What can you do this week? This month? This year?

Asking yourself, "What is my prison?" isn't just about identifying the bars around you; it's about realizing that the door might just be unlocked. And here's the real kicker: sometimes, you've had the key all along. It's about choosing to unlock the door, step out, and breathe the fresh air of freedom. Keep pushing, keep growing, and let's break out of these prisons together.

Chapter 2: The Power of Perspective

Seeing Things Differently to Tackle Life's Problems

When you hit rock bottom, you've got two choices: stay there, or start climbing up. It all begins with perspective, because how you see things shapes how you live through them. Now, let's be real—it's not easy to shift your view when you feel like life's pinned you down. But if you decide to change the way you look at the struggle, everything can start to shift with it.

Understanding Chaos as Part of Life Prison handed me a front-row ticket to chaos. Every single day, the walls reminded me how much I'd lost. It would have been easy to spiral into bitterness, but here's the deal: chaos, just like peace, is part of the game. Once I accepted that life was full of storms and setbacks, I made a decision to find my balance within the chaos, not against it. Instead of expecting smooth sailing, I learned to navigate the rough waters.

Maybe for you, chaos is different. It might be a job loss, a breakup, or a family mess. But to keep it real, the sooner you accept that chaos is part of the ride, the sooner you're ready to deal with it. Instead of fighting the storm, learn to steer through it.

Reframing Challenges as Growth Opportunities When I finally accepted the chaos, I started asking myself a different question: What can I gain here? Prison could take my freedom, but it couldn't stop me from growing. I took on each day as a lesson, whether I was learning to write or mentoring someone who was at rock bottom, too.

For you, reframing could mean shifting "Why me?" to "What's in it for me?" This switch doesn't change the challenge, but it changes how you handle it. Here's what's up: every setback can be a setup for growth if you choose to see it that way.

Practicing Gratitude in Hard Times Gratitude wasn't exactly on my mind at first, but as time passed, I found myself grateful for small things—the fact that I still had my health, my mind, and the ability to connect with others. Keeping it real—gratitude became my quiet rebellion against the darkness. I'd sit in my cell and find things to be thankful for, no matter how tiny. Those moments gave me something to hold onto and looking ahead.

For you, gratitude could look different. It might be a daily habit of listing what you're thankful for, even on the hardest days. Here's the deal:

gratitude won't erase the pain, but it can shift your focus to what you still have, and that can make all the difference.

Exercise for the Reader: Perspective Journal This chapter is about challenging your view, so here's a small exercise to try:

1. **Identify a challenge you're facing. Write it down.**
2. **List three ways to reframe it. Ask yourself what you could learn from it, what opportunity it holds, or what small things you're grateful for.**
3. **Reflect on how changing your perspective affects how you feel.**

Changing your perspective isn't about pretending everything's perfect. It's about finding strength to face the pain and **come up** stronger. We all get dealt a hand, but **how we play it** is what sets us apart.

Chapter 3: Facing the Fall

Handling Setbacks Head-On Without Fear

When life as you know it crashes down, the first reaction is usually to avoid the pain, shut it out, pretend it didn't hit you as hard as it did. But let's be real: running from pain only fuels it. The only way out of pain is through it. Facing it head-on lets you see it for what it really is—a moment in your story, but not the whole story. To bounce back, you've got to sit with it, feel it, and then let it go.

Acknowledging Your Pain Pain isn't just a fleeting feeling; it can linger and be overtaking. When I lost my freedom, I came face-to-face with a level of pain that stripped me bare. No more fancy titles or deals—family times—just me, four walls, under the weight of all my choices. I could've spent every day denying the hurt, but here's what's up: pain doesn't disappear just because you ignore it. Instead, I forced myself to look straight at it. I felt the anger, the regret, the sorrow. It wasn't easy, but facing it taught me that pain doesn't have to define you forever.

In your own life, whatever the challenge, give yourself the freedom to feel it. Feel the sadness, the frustration, the pain, even the anger if it's there. To keep it real, suppressing pain only buries it deeper, but takes away its power. That's the first step to dealing with it, and healing.

The Art of Self-Compassion One of the hardest lessons I had to learn was how to be kind to myself. There were countless moments I wanted to beat myself up for every decision that led me to prison. I thought self-compassion was for the weak. But here's the deal: I had to become my own friend, treating myself like I would anyone else struggling. Compassion isn't about excusing your mistakes—it's about realizing that we all have setbacks and we're all worthy of forgiveness, especially self-forgiveness, and grace.

Self-compassion is a game-changer. Imagine how you'd talk to a friend going through the same thing. Try giving yourself that same understanding and kindness. What's up with that inner critic, anyway? Sometimes, it's your biggest enemy. Silence the negative chatter and see what happens.

Seeking Support

Even though I was behind bars, I wasn't entirely alone. I connected with men who were struggling just like me. Finding support became a lifeline, something that reminded me we were all carrying heavy burdens.

In your own life, whether it's talking to family, a friend, or a professional, don't shy away from reaching out. Let's be real—asking for support doesn't make you weak. It shows you're strong enough to know when you need someone to lean on. Connection is a lifeline, one that can help you through the darkest days.

Exercise for the Fighter: Self-Compassion Practice This chapter is all about facing your pain with compassion, so here's a quick exercise:

1. **Write a letter to yourself as if you were talking to a friend. Be real, be kind, and offer support.**
2. **List three qualities you respect about yourself—no matter how small.**
3. **Reflect on how showing yourself kindness feels. Does it make facing the hard stuff a little lighter?**

Facing the fall isn't about feeling better overnight. It's about opening up to healing, knowing that the pain is real but it doesn't have to stay forever. Each day, you're choosing resilience, and that choice adds up.

Chapter 4: Rising from the Ashes

Handling Setbacks Head-On Without Fear

When it feels like life has burned everything down, it's hard to imagine anything good coming from it. Let's keep it real: rebuilding isn't a quick fix. Rising from the ashes doesn't mean trying to get back to who you were before. It's about creating something new—something more grounded, more real, and often, stronger than you ever thought possible.

Harnessing the Power of Self-Reflection Hitting rock bottom gives you one tool that's hard to get anywhere else: self-reflection. I had all the time in the world to look back, not to beat myself up but to understand where I went wrong. Alone in my cell, I confronted the decisions that led me there, taking them apart and learning what I needed to change.

For you, self-reflection might not look quite as intense. Maybe it's a quiet moment at the end of the day or a journal entry where you're honest with yourself. Here's what's up: self-reflection isn't about regret—it's about clarity. It's like looking in the mirror, not to judge but to understand where you want to go next.

Setting Achievable Goals Once I had a clearer sense of where I was, I began setting small, realistic goals. In prison, my goals were humble: learning a skill, finishing a book, lor writing a chapter. Each goal was a small step forward, something that kept me from stagnating.

If you're starting over, set goals that feel doable, even if they seem small. You're not aiming for perfection—just progress. Goals as simple as "read for 10 minutes a day", "reach out to one friend", or "make a new friend" can be powerful. To keep it real, it's not the size of the goal but the consistency that counts. Every step forward builds momentum, and before you know it, you'll look back and see how far you've come.

Embracing Action, Even When It's Hard Starting over means taking action, even on days when it feels pointless. I had moments where getting up felt like a laborious effort, but staying down wasn't an option. I kept moving, day after day, whether it was reading, writing, or just connecting with someone. Here's the deal: action, no matter how small, keeps you going. Little by little, it builds endurance and strength.

For you, taking action could be as simple as getting out of bed and facing the day. Take one step, and then another. You might not see progress immediately, but every small action is a step toward your comeback.

Exercise for the Reader: Small Steps to Big Change Since rebuilding is all about small, consistent steps, here's a quick exercise to get you started:

1. **Choose an area in your life where you want to see improvement. Write it down.**
2. **Set three small goals that feel achievable over the next month. Think of them as steps, not leaps.**
3. **Reflect weekly on your progress. Every action counts, no matter how small.**

Rising from the ashes isn't about grand gestures or quick results. It's about the courage to start and keep going, celebrating every small win. Over time, those small wins become the backbone of your next chapter.

Chapter 5: Reclaiming Your Power

Taking Back Control of Your Life

When life throws you off track, it can feel like your sense of control is gone. Here's the deal: the power to choose how you respond and who you'll become is still yours, even when circumstances seem to say otherwise. Reclaiming your power isn't about controlling everything that happens. It's about recognizing your ability to decide what comes next, even when you feel like you've got no options left.

Owning Your Choices One of the hardest things to do in tough times is to take ownership of your choices. When I was facing my own situation, it would've been easy to blame the system, blame others, or let bitterness settle in. But to keep it real, the only way forward was to own up to where I was and accept the role my decisions played in getting there.

Taking ownership isn't about beating yourself up. It's about standing in the reality of your choices so you can move on with clarity. When you own your choices, you reclaim the power that seemed lost. You can say, "Yeah, I got myself here, but I can get myself out, too." What's up with that level of accountability? It's freeing. It lets you take the wheel, ready to steer toward something better.

Redefining Your Value In tough times, it's easy to question your worth. You start wondering if any of it matters—your work, your relationships, even your dreams. Here's what's up: your value doesn't disappear when you're down. You're not defined by the lows or the mistakes. Your worth is innate, something that no setback can erase.

During my darkest days, I had to remind myself that my circumstances didn't define me. I was still the same person with the same potential to thrive and rise again. The key is redefining what success and value look like for you, on your own terms. Remember that your worth is yours alone, not determined by your worst decision or lowest moment.

Embracing Accountability as Strength Owning your power also means holding yourself accountable—not in a way that drags you down, but one that lifts you up. Accountability isn't about self-punishment; it's about choosing to stay responsible for what you want to achieve next. In prison, I learned to hold myself accountable for every small action. When you do that, you begin to build trust with yourself, and that trust is powerful.

When you make a choice, own it. When you set a goal, keep yourself to it. This kind of accountability is empowering. It reminds you that you're not just surviving—you're actively creating the life you want, one decision at a time.

Exercise for the Reader: Power Reclamation Checklist To start reclaiming your power, try this quick exercise:

1. **Identify one area where you feel powerless. Write it down.**
2. **Pinpoint one choice you can make right now to improve it, no matter how small.**
3. **Commit to an action that reinforces your value—something that reminds you of your worth, even if it's just telling yourself, "I deserve better."**

Reclaiming your power isn't about waiting for a perfect moment. It's about deciding, right here and now, to step back into the driver's seat and move toward what you want.

CHAPTER 6: FINDING PURPOSE IN THE PROCESS DISCOVERING MEANING IN EVERY STEP YOU TAKE

When life throws you a knockdown punch, purpose can feel like the first thing to disappear. Suddenly, everything you worked for, believed in, or counted on seems shaken or gone. But let's be real: purpose doesn't have to be tied to just one achievement or dream. Sometimes, it's the process of rebuilding and learning that reveals a purpose you never even knew was there.

The Power of Daily Purpose In my hardest days, purpose became something I had to rediscover, one day at a time. I couldn't rely on the bigger goals or grand ambitions anymore, so I learned to find purpose in the simple, daily actions. To keep it real, some days, my only purpose was to make it through that day, to read, to write, to grow a little more than the day before.

Purpose doesn't have to be some grand, life-altering revelation. It can be found in the small, meaningful actions that add up. Maybe it's just the decision to learn something new, to be kind, or to connect with others. Every day brings a chance to find purpose in the little things.

Turning Setbacks into Fuel A setback can knock the wind out of you. But it can also be the spark that pushes you toward something you never considered before. For me, those moments of loss and isolation forced me to dig deep, to see what I was really made of. Here's what's up: setbacks aren't the end of the road. They can be the fuel that propels you toward a new, beneficial direction.

When a setback hits, ask yourself how it might fuel your growth. Instead of seeing it as an obstacle, try to look at it as an opportunity to reroute and discover new potential. The road to purpose often takes you through detours you never saw coming.

Building Resilience Through Service One of the most powerful ways I found purpose was through helping others, even if it was just in small ways. I found that when I focused on helping the men around me, I felt more connected, more whole. Service has a way of reminding us that we're all in this together, that we can thrive better when we lift each other up.

For you, finding purpose might mean looking outside yourself and seeing how you can support others. It doesn't have to be big or flashy; even the smallest acts of kindness can bring purpose and light back into your life. What's up with that? It's a reminder that purpose is sometimes found in the moments when we're just there for each other.

Exercise for the Reader: Purpose Discovery Practice If you're ready to start uncovering purpose, try this:

1. **List three small actions that make you feel fulfilled. These can be as simple as connecting with a friend, learning something new, or spending time in nature.**
2. **Set one daily intention that aligns with these actions, something you can work toward each day.**
3. **Reflect weekly on how these small, purposeful actions impact your life.**

Finding purpose is a process, one that takes time, reflection, and openness. But each small action you take brings you closer to a purpose that feels true to you.

Chapter 7: The Strength in Vulnerability

Finding True Strength by Being Open

When the world tells you to "be strong," it's easy to interpret that as "don't show weakness" or "don't let them see you struggle." But here's the deal: real strength isn't about putting up walls or pretending you're invincible. True resilience often comes from letting yourself be vulnerable, owning your struggles, and opening up about what you're going through.

Redefining Strength In my journey, I learned that strength and vulnerability aren't opposites—they go hand in hand. To let people see my pain, to admit that I was hurting or that I didn't have all the answers, took more courage than pretending to be unaffected. Let's be real: the act of letting down your guard isn't about weakness; it's about being strong enough to be genuine.

When you open up, even just a little, you're creating space for real connection. Vulnerability isn't about dumping all your issues on others; it's about acknowledging that you're human and that sometimes you don't have it all together. And that's okay.

Embracing Help as a Power Move I used to think that asking for help was a sign of weakness. But here's what's up: knowing when to reach out is actually one of the strongest moves you can make. During my toughest times, leaning on others taught me that we're not meant to do everything alone. And sometimes, the very thing you need most to move forward is a little help from someone else.

Allowing others to help isn't about depending on them to fix things. It's about creating a support system—a group of people who can lift you up, help you gain perspective, and remind you of your strength when you're struggling to see it. That's what real resilience looks like: knowing when to stand tall on your own and when to lean on people who care or can relate.

Exercise for the Reader: Vulnerability Practice To start building strength through vulnerability, try this:

1. **Think of one area where you've been struggling. Write it down.**

2. **Identify one person you trust who might understand. This could be a friend, family member, or even a counselor.**
3. **Open up in a small way about your struggle—just enough to let them in. Notice how it feels to share and to be supported.**

This practice isn't about oversharing. It's about recognizing that vulnerability can be a path to strength and that letting people in can bring healing.

Chapter 8: Building Your Resilience Toolbox

Gearing Up with Tools for Tough Times

Resilience isn't something you just decide to have one day. It's built over time, with every setback, every challenge, and every time you choose to get back up. To keep it real, resilience is like a muscle, and the more you work at it, the stronger it gets. Building a resilience toolbox—your own set of strategies to lean on when times get tough—can make all the difference.

Establishing Healthy Habits Resilience isn't just about big, heroic actions; it's also built on small, everyday habits. During my journey, I learned that the routines I created—whether it was reading, writing, or exercising—gave me structure and a sense of purpose. What's up with that? These daily habits became anchors, things I could count on to ground me even when everything else felt shaky.

Healthy habits don't have to be intense or time-consuming. Find small actions that add up and bring a sense of control back into your day. It could be as simple as starting each day with a goal, a moment of gratitude, or an exercise routine. When you commit to these little actions, you're reinforcing your resilience, one day at a time.

Practicing Mindfulness and Letting Go Mindfulness taught me to stay present, to stop dwelling on the "what ifs" or the regrets of the past. Here's the deal: holding onto negative thoughts or obsessing over what went wrong only drains your energy. Letting go of that mental clutter frees you up to focus on the present and build for the future.

Mindfulness isn't just sitting in meditation (though it can be!). It's a mindset, a decision to be fully here in the moment. Try focusing on your breath, noticing your surroundings, or even taking a break to reset when you feel overwhelmed. Each time you practice letting go, you're giving yourself more space to thrive.

Celebrating Small Wins

Resilience is also about recognizing and celebrating progress, no matter how small. When I achieved even the smallest goal, I took a moment to appreciate it. Over time, these small wins became fuel for the bigger goals.

Let's be real: life doesn't give out trophies for getting through tough times, so you've got to celebrate yourself.

No matter how insignificant a win might feel, take the time to acknowledge it. For me, it was often the small moments of progress that built confidence and reinforced that I was capable of coming through, again and again.

Exercise for the Reader: Resilience Tools Check-In To start building your resilience toolbox, try this:

1. **Identify three habits that help you feel more grounded. Write them down and commit to practicing them daily.**
2. **List one mindfulness practice you're willing to try this week —whether it's deep breathing, a short meditation, or a moment of gratitude.**
3. **Note down a recent small win and celebrate it. Take a moment to reflect on what this win means for your journey.**

Building resilience isn't about grand gestures; it's about stacking small steps and consistent habits that keep you strong when life gets hard.

Chapter 9: The Power of Patience

Learning to Stay Calm While You Wait

Let's dive into patience—not just as a virtue, but as a game-changer in tackling life's curveballs. Here’s the real deal: life doesn’t care about our timelines, but mastering patience helps us see beyond immediate frustrations to potential opportunities.

Cultivating a Patient Mindset Patience starts in your mind. When I was in prison, every day was a test. I could either let frustration take over, or I could use the time to my advantage. I chose the latter. I treated my sentence like a marathon, focusing on endurance and personal growth, because real healing and growth can't be rushed.

Think about your own setbacks. When things don’t go your way, try to see these slowdowns as pauses, not full stops. These moments are chances to gather your thoughts and strength, not just wasted time. Viewing delays as opportunities can transform a frustrating wait into a strategic pause.

Practicing Patience Daily Patience is a skill that gets stronger with practice. Start small: if you're stuck in traffic, think of it as a chance to unwind or explore a new playlist, rather than a nuisance. These moments of patience build your resilience for bigger challenges.

Every moment you choose patience, you’re not just passing time—you're enhancing your life. It helps you build resilience, enjoy the present more, and reduce stress on yourself and others.

Patience and Progress Progress rarely happens in a straight line. It’s easy to get discouraged by slow movement, but patience helps you appreciate the small wins—those tiny, often overlooked steps that are crucial for long-term success.

Focusing on gradual improvement, rather than instant results, leads to more substantial and enduring achievements. Each small victory or lesson, however minor, is a step forward.

Patience is more than just waiting; it's about how you wait and what you do with that time. Embracing patience is part of the journey towards a happier, more fulfilled life. Keep pushing, keep growing, and let patience guide you.

Exercise for the Reader: 1. Reflection: Take a moment to reflect on a recent situation where you felt impatient. Write down what triggered your impatience and how you reacted. Now, reimagine the scenario with a patient mindset—how could the outcome have been different?

2. Gratitude Practice: For one week, keep a daily gratitude journal. Each day, write down at least three things you're thankful for. Try to focus on different aspects each day. Notice any changes in your mood or outlook by the end of the week.

3. Patience Challenge: Choose one area in your life where you usually lack patience. It could be dealing with traffic, waiting in lines, or handling slow responses from others. For the next month, consciously apply patience each time this situation occurs. Take note of any differences in how you feel and react.

These exercises are designed to strengthen your patience, helping you to cultivate a more patient and proactive approach to life's challenges.

Chapter 10: Building Inner Strength

Developing Unshakable Confidence from Within

Inner strength isn't something you're born with; it's something you build over time. When life knocks you down, the way you respond to it makes all the difference. To keep it real, building inner strength is a process—a mix of discipline, self-belief, and a refusal to stay down.

Cultivating Self-Belief One of the hardest things to maintain, especially when everything feels stacked against you, is self-belief. But here's the thing: you don't have to believe you'll be successful at everything; you just have to believe in your ability to keep going. Let's be real—there were days I didn't believe in much, but I always believed in my ability to push forward.

If you're feeling like you're lacking in self-belief, start small. Remind yourself of past challenges you've overcome. Remember times when you got through what felt impossible. The more you reinforce these memories, the more you build that inner strength.

Embracing Discipline Inner strength isn't about motivation; it's about discipline. Motivation can come and go, but discipline is what keeps you going when the going gets tough. In prison, discipline was my best friend. It was discipline that got me up each day, kept me on a routine, and helped me make the most of my time. Here's what's up: when you're disciplined, you're taking control of your actions regardless of how you feel.

Discipline doesn't mean setting impossible standards or working yourself into the ground. It's about creating habits that support you, day in and day out. Start by setting a small goal—a daily routine or a simple habit—and stick to it. Over time, these small acts of discipline add up to a lot of inner strength.

Tapping into Resilience Inner strength and resilience go hand in hand. Resilience is your ability to bounce back, to rise up after you've fallen. It's not about avoiding hardship; it's about being able to face it and keep moving forward. Resilience is what allows you to grow stronger with each setback, to turn every stumble into a setup for your next comeback.

Here's the deal: resilience is built in the small moments—each time you get back up, each time you choose not to quit. Think of each challenge as training, each setback as a stepping stone. With each bounce back, you're proving to yourself that no matter what life throws your way, you have what it takes to get back up and keep moving.

Exercise for the Reader: Building Inner Strength To start building your inner strength, try this exercise:

1. **Think of one small goal you want to accomplish this week. Write it down and commit to it.**
2. **Reflect on a past challenge you've overcome and remind yourself of the strength it took.**
3. **Set a daily discipline practice—something you'll commit to even when it's hard.**

These small acts of self-belief, discipline, and resilience will start to build a foundation of inner strength that can support you through whatever comes your way.

CHAPTER 11: FINDING PURPOSE IN THE PAIN TURNING HARD TIMES INTO PERSONAL GROWTH

Sometimes life throws you curveballs so intense they shake you to the core, making you wonder why things happen the way they do. To keep it real, I asked myself "why" a lot. Why was I here? Why did things turn out this way? But through the struggle, I found a surprising truth: purpose often rises from pain.

Turning Adversity into Fuel Pain can either pull you down or push you forward—it all depends on what you do with it. When I found myself at rock bottom, I realized that, even in my darkest days, I had the choice to make something meaningful out of it. Here's the deal: when you start looking at your challenges as opportunities for growth, they lose some of their sting.

So, take a good look at the hard stuff in your life. Instead of letting it keep you down, consider how you can use it to fuel your purpose. Maybe it's learning something about yourself, maybe it's helping others going through similar struggles, or maybe it's turning that pain into something powerful. Purpose doesn't have to be some grand idea; it can be as simple as using what you've learned to make someone else's life a bit better.

Finding Your "Why"

Purpose doesn't just fall into your lap. You have to dig for it, to ask yourself the tough questions. Let's be real: finding your "why" takes time, but it gives you a reason to keep going when life gets rough. For me, that purpose became clear over time—mentoring others, sharing my story, and hopefully inspiring a few people to bounce back from their own setbacks.

Take a moment to ask yourself what lights you up, what motivates you even when things are hard. Think of what gives your life meaning, and don't worry if it takes a while to uncover. Your "why" is the anchor that holds you steady, no matter what comes your way.

Embracing the Journey Finding purpose is a journey, not a destination. Here's what's up: purpose is something you build every day, with every choice you make. It might start as a small spark, but over time, it can grow into something powerful enough to keep you going through the toughest of times. Embrace the journey, let your purpose evolve, and trust that each step is leading you somewhere meaningful.

Exercise for the Reader: Discovering Your Purpose Here's a quick exercise to start exploring your purpose:

1. **List three challenges you've faced in life and write down one thing each taught you.**
2. **Think about a way you can use those lessons to make a difference, no matter how small.**
3. **Reflect on how it feels to imagine that purpose taking shape. Does it give you a sense of motivation or meaning?**

Finding purpose in your pain may not change your circumstances, but it can change how you live within them—and that shift can be the most powerful move of all.

Chapter 12: Embracing Change

Rolling with the Punches to Thrive

Change is tough. It's uncomfortable, it's unpredictable, and let's be real, it's downright scary sometimes. But resisting change only keeps you stuck. Embracing it? That's where the growth happens.

Redefining Change as Growth We often think of change as something that happens to us, but here's the deal: change is also something we can create. During my time behind bars, everything about my life changed, but I soon learned that if I leaned into it, I could redefine who I was. I stopped seeing change as an enemy and started seeing it as a chance to grow in ways I never thought possible.

Whatever changes you're going through, try looking at them as opportunities instead of obstacles. When you see change as a chance to grow, it loses some of its intimidation. Instead of resisting, lean into it and let it shape you into something stronger.

Letting Go of the Past

Embracing change often means letting go of the past, and let's be real, that's not easy. But hanging on to what used to be only holds you back from what could be. I had to let go of the life I knew before and embrace the new reality I was living. It was hard, but it was also liberating. Letting go of who you used to be creates space for who you're becoming.

Take a look at the things you're holding on to that might be keeping you stuck. Letting go doesn't mean forgetting; it just means freeing yourself from the weight of what can't be changed. When you release the past, you open yourself up to everything new that's waiting for you.

Accepting What You Can't Control Life is unpredictable, and here's what's up: there are just some things you can't control. But there's power in acceptance. When you stop fighting the things you can't change, you make space for focusing on what you can. This shift in focus can

bring a sense of peace and clarity, allowing you to approach each new challenge with an open mind.

Accepting what's out of your hands frees up your energy to work on what's within your control. Instead of stressing over what you can't change, channel that energy into areas where you can make a difference.

Exercise for the Reader: Embracing Change Practice Here's an exercise to help you start embracing change:

1. **Write down one change you're currently facing and describe how it makes you feel.**
2. **Identify one positive outcome this change could bring, even if it's small.**
3. **List one thing you need to let go of to move forward, and commit to releasing it.**

Embracing change isn't easy, but it's worth it. When you let go of resistance, you make room for transformation—and that's where true growth happens.

CHAPTER 13: LETTING GO OF SHAME AND GUILT DROPPING EMOTIONAL WEIGHT TO MOVE FORWARD

Shame and guilt have a way of chaining you to the past. They're like heavy weights that keep you from moving forward. To keep it real, I carried those weights for a long time, feeling like I'd never shake them off. But letting go of shame and guilt isn't about pretending nothing happened. It's about deciding you won't let the past hold you back anymore.

Turning Shame into Strength Shame can feel like it's there to punish you, but here's the deal: it can also become a source of strength. When I finally faced my shame head-on, I realized that my story, with all its mistakes, could actually help others. My lowest moments could become the foundation of something better if I chose to use them that way.

In your own life, think about how you might turn shame into something powerful. Maybe it's using what you've learned to help someone else, or maybe it's sharing your story to inspire others. Turning shame into strength isn't about ignoring the past; it's about transforming it into something that serves you.

Practicing Self-Forgiveness Letting go of guilt means forgiving yourself, which is easier said than done. Forgiveness doesn't mean you're excusing what happened—it means you're choosing to release the hold it has on you. Self-forgiveness is about acknowledging that you're human, that you've learned, and that you deserve a chance to move forward.

Here's what's up: forgiving yourself is one of the most freeing things you can do. Think of it as an act of compassion, something that allows you to grow without dragging the weight of guilt with you. Let yourself move on, knowing that every step forward is a choice to become the person you want to be.

Exercise for the Reader: Self-Forgiveness Letter Try this exercise if you're struggling to let go of shame or guilt:

1. **Write a letter to yourself as if you were a friend. Acknowledge your mistakes, but offer forgiveness.**
2. **Reflect on what you've learned from those experiences, and remind yourself that you've grown.**
3. **End with a commitment to let go of the past and focus on building your future.**

Letting go of shame and guilt doesn't erase what happened, but it does free you to focus on what's next. Each day is a new chance to step into the life you're creating.

CHAPTER 14: EMBRACING A MINDSET OF GROWTH SEEING SUCCESS AS ALWAYS GETTING BETTER

When you start seeing challenges as opportunities to grow, life changes. Here's the deal: a growth mindset isn't about pretending everything is great. It's about recognizing that, no matter what life throws at you, there's something you can gain from it. Embracing a mindset of growth allows you to bounce back from setbacks, learn from mistakes, and keep pushing forward.

Shifting from Fixed to Growth A fixed mindset says, "I'm not good at this, so I'll never be good at it." A growth mindset says, "I might not be good at this yet, but I can get better." During my journey, I had to shift my thinking from seeing challenges as failures to seeing them as opportunities to improve. Let's be real: shifting to a growth mindset doesn't mean you won't still struggle. It just means you'll see struggles as part of the process.

In your life, start by noticing when you're being hard on yourself, when you're saying, "I can't." Replace that with, "I can't do it *yet*." Embrace the idea that growth is always possible, and that each challenge is just another chance to get stronger.

Setting Goals Focused on Growth Goals focused on growth aren't about perfection; they're about progress. For me, small goals—like learning a new skill or pushing myself to write each day—became stepping stones to a larger sense of purpose. When you set goals based on growth, each milestone you reach adds to your confidence.

Set goals that push you just a little outside your comfort zone, goals that make you stretch but still feel achievable. Each time you reach one, you'll be building a habit of growth. And what's up with that? You'll start to feel capable of facing anything, one step at a time.

Embracing the Power of "Yet"

One of the best parts of a growth mindset is the word "yet." When you say, "I'm not there *yet*," you're reminding yourself that the journey isn't over and that progress is still possible. Adding "yet" to your vocabulary changes your perspective. It's a reminder that you're on a journey, and just because you haven't reached your destination doesn't mean you won't get there.

Every time you face a challenge or feel like giving up, remember that "yet" is still in play. You're still growing, still learning, and still moving forward.

Exercise for the Reader: Growth Mindset Challenge Try this exercise to start embracing a mindset of growth:

1. **Identify a challenge you're facing and write down how it makes you feel.**
2. **Add the word "yet" to any negative thoughts (e.g., "I can't do this" becomes "I can't do this *yet*").**
3. **Set one small goal that challenges you to grow, something you can work toward over the next week.**

Adopting a growth mindset doesn't mean you'll never struggle, but it does mean you'll see each struggle as a step forward. Embrace the journey, knowing that with each effort, you're getting closer to the person you want to be.

CHAPTER 15: THE FREEDOM TO REDEFINE SUCCESS SETTING YOUR OWN GOALS FOR HAPPINESS

For a long time, success meant climbing the ladder, making deals, and reaching for more. But when life hit me hard, I realized that those markers of success don't mean much if they're not backed by real purpose and fulfillment. Here's what's up: true success isn't about meeting everyone else's expectations; it's about living a life that feels right to you.

Defining Success on Your Own Terms The world will tell you that success looks a certain way—money, status, or fame. But to keep it real, none of that matters if you're not genuinely happy or fulfilled. After losing so much, I realized that success needed to mean something deeper. For me, it became about peace of mind, living in line with my values, and finding purpose in what I do.

In your own life, think about what success means to you. Maybe it's a fulfilling career, maybe it's being there for your family, or maybe it's simply waking up each day with a sense of contentment. When you define success on your terms, you set yourself free from everyone else's expectations and create a path that feels true to you.

Setting Goals That Align with Your Values Redefining success means setting goals that align with what matters most to you. It's not about impressing others; it's about living a life that reflects your core values. During my journey, I learned that success was about more than external achievements. It was about creating a life that felt honest, purposeful, and meaningful to me.

If you're redefining success, start by identifying your core values. What matters most to you? Set goals that align with those values, even if they don’t look flashy or impressive to others. Here’s the deal: success isn’t about what others think; it’s about how you feel at the end of the day.

Embracing Progress Over Perfection Redefining success also means letting go of perfection. Life isn’t a straight line, and success doesn’t mean you’ll never make mistakes. Real success is found in progress, in moving forward even when things get messy. When I stopped striving for perfection and started focusing on progress, I felt a freedom I’d never experienced before.

Instead of aiming for perfect, aim for consistent growth. Embrace each small step as a win, and remember that every bit of progress brings you closer to the life you want. Success is a journey, not a destination. Keep moving forward, and let go of the need to have it all figured out.

Exercise for the Reader: Success Re-Defined Here’s an exercise to help you redefine success:

1. **Write down three values that feel central to who you are.**
2. **Reflect on how these values can guide your definition of success.**
3. **Set one goal that aligns with these values and represents success for you, not anyone else.**

Redefining success on your own terms gives you the freedom to create a life that feels fulfilling and genuine. Each step you take toward this version of success is a step toward living a life that’s truly yours.

CHAPTER 16: THE POWER OF LETTING GO FINDING FREEDOM BY RELEASING THE PAST

Letting go is one of the hardest things to do. We hold onto old ideas, past mistakes, and even pain because they're familiar. But let's be real: letting go is the only way to move forward. When you let go of what's holding you back, you create space for something new to grow.

Releasing Old Beliefs

Sometimes, the hardest thing to let go of is an old belief. We all carry around ideas about who we are, what we can or can't do, and what life "should" look like. But when those beliefs stop serving you, it's time to let them go. For me, letting go of certain beliefs was a turning point. I realized that just because something had been true in the past didn't mean it had to define my future.

Take a look at the beliefs you're holding onto. Are there any that no longer serve you? Letting go of outdated beliefs isn't easy, but it's freeing. Here's the deal: when you release what no longer fits, you make room for new possibilities.

Forgiving Yourself and Others Forgiveness is one of the most powerful acts of letting go. Holding onto grudges or self-blame only weighs you down. I had to forgive myself for my mistakes and forgive others for the hurt they caused me. Forgiveness isn't about excusing what happened; it's about choosing to let go of the anger and pain.

In your own life, consider what or who you need to forgive. Maybe it's yourself, maybe it's someone who hurt you. Forgiveness is a gift you give yourself, freeing you to live without the weight of resentment. What's up with that? It's simple: you deserve peace - forgiveness helps you find it.

Embracing the Unknown

Letting go often means stepping into the unknown, and that can be scary. But to keep it real, the unknown is where growth happens. Embracing the unknown doesn't mean you won't feel fear—it means you'll move forward in spite of it. For me, letting go of the familiar opened doors to new perspectives and experiences I never expected.

If you're facing the unknown, remind yourself that growth often comes from uncertainty. Letting go of the need for control allows you to adapt, evolve, and discover new paths. Trust yourself to handle whatever comes next, and embrace the freedom that comes with stepping into the unknown.

Exercise for the Reader: The Letting Go Practice To start letting go of what's holding you back, try this:

1. **Identify one belief, memory, or resentment you're holding onto.**
2. **Reflect on what's keeping you attached to it and how letting it go might benefit you.**
3. **Make a commitment to release it, and take a small action toward that commitment.**

Letting go isn't about losing; it's about creating space for something better. Each time you let go of what's weighing you down, you make room for new growth, peace, and purpose.

CHAPTER 17: EMBRACING CHANGE AS AN OPPORTUNITY VIEWING NEW STARTS AS CHANCES TO GROW

Change is inevitable, but how you respond to it is what shapes your life. In prison, I learned that change wasn't my enemy—it was an opportunity, a chance to reinvent myself. To keep it real, you can't stop change, but you can choose to make it work for you.

Seeing Change as Growth When you start looking at change as an opportunity to grow, you begin to see it differently. I could've seen my circumstances as the end, but instead, I chose to see them as a period of transformation. Here's the deal: every change brings with it the potential for growth, even when it doesn't feel that way at first.

Whatever changes you're going through, try shifting your perspective. Instead of resisting, ask yourself how this change might help you grow or teach you something valuable. It won't make the change easy, but it will make it meaningful.

Letting Go of Control

One of the hardest parts of embracing change is letting go of control. I couldn’t control the world around me, but I could control my response to it. Here’s what’s up: trying to control everything only brings stress. When you let go of control, you give yourself the freedom to adapt and grow.

If you’re struggling with change, take a step back. Focus on what’s within your control—your actions, your mindset, and your responses. Everything else? Let it go. When you release control, you create space for new possibilities to unfold.

Exercise for the Reader: Embracing Change Exercise To start embracing change, try this:

1. **Write down one change you’re currently facing.**
2. **List one way this change could help you grow or bring something positive into your life.**
3. **Reflect on what you can control and make a commitment to focus on that.**

Embracing change isn’t about avoiding the discomfort; it’s about finding purpose within it. Each change brings a new opportunity to grow into the person you want to become.

CHAPTER 18: LEARNING FROM MISTAKES WITHOUT DWELLING ON REGRET MOVING FORWARD BY LEARNING, NOT LAMENTING

Mistakes are a part of life, but carrying regret doesn't have to be. We all make choices we wish we could take back, but let's be real: dwelling on regret only keeps you stuck. Learning from your mistakes and moving forward is the best way to honor your journey.

Turning Mistakes into Lessons Every mistake I made taught me something valuable. Instead of letting regret weigh me down, I started seeing my mistakes as stepping stones. Here's the deal: when you learn from your mistakes, they become a part of your growth instead of something that holds you back.

Think about the mistakes you're carrying. Ask yourself what each one has taught you. Turning your mistakes into lessons is a way to reclaim your power, to use the past as a guide rather than a burden.

Practicing Self-Forgiveness Self-forgiveness is crucial if you want to move forward. I had to forgive myself for the choices that led me to prison, and that wasn't easy. But here's what's up: holding onto guilt only keeps you from growing. Self-forgiveness doesn't mean ignoring what happened; it means accepting that you're human, that you've learned, and that you deserve a fresh start.

If you're struggling to forgive yourself, take it one step at a time. Remind yourself that mistakes don't define you. Forgiveness is a choice to release guilt and focus on becoming the person you’re working to be.

Exercise for the Reader: Releasing Regret Practice If you’re ready to release regret, try this:

1. **Think of a mistake you still feel regretful about.**
2. **Identify one lesson that mistake taught you.**
3. **Write a forgiveness statement for yourself, committing to let go of the regret.**

Releasing regret frees you to focus on the present and build a better future. Mistakes don’t have to be permanent weights—they can be lessons that lead you forward.

Chapter 19: Cultivating Inner Peace

Finding Calm in Chaotic Surroundings

Life can be chaotic, and finding inner peace isn't always easy. But to keep it real, peace isn't about escaping life's challenges—it's about learning to stay grounded no matter what comes your way. Inner peace is something you build from within, a sense of calm that carries you through every storm.

Accepting Impermanence One of the keys to inner peace is accepting that everything is temporary. Situations change, people come and go, and emotions rise and fall. Here's what's up: peace doesn't mean everything is perfect; it means you're okay with the ebb and flow of life.

Accepting impermanence frees you from the fear of losing control. When you embrace the idea that nothing lasts forever, you allow yourself to be fully present, to enjoy the good moments, and to endure the tough ones, knowing that they too will pass.

Practicing Mindfulness Mindfulness is one of the most powerful tools for finding peace. In my journey, mindfulness helped me focus on the present instead of worrying about the past or future. Here's the deal: mindfulness isn't about clearing your mind; it's about observing your thoughts without judgment.

Try practicing mindfulness each day, even if it's just a few minutes. Take a deep breath, focus on the here and now, and let go of any thoughts that pull you away. The more you practice, the easier it becomes to tap into that inner calm.

Embracing Self-Compassion Inner peace also comes from treating yourself with kindness. Life is hard enough without beating yourself up over every mistake or flaw. Let's be real: self-compassion is essential. When you're gentle with yourself, you create a foundation of peace that helps you stay grounded.

If you find yourself being self-critical, take a step back. Imagine how you'd talk to a friend going through the same situation, and offer yourself that same understanding. Embracing self-compassion lets you navigate life's ups and downs with grace.

Exercise for the Reader: Cultivating Inner Peace To start building inner peace, try this:

1. **Set aside five minutes each day to practice mindfulness. Focus on your breathing and let go of any thoughts.**
2. **Identify one area where you're hard on yourself, and practice self-compassion in that area.**
3. **Reflect on impermanence by noting one recent event that came and went, reminding yourself that life is constantly flowing.**

Cultivating inner peace is a lifelong journey, but each step you take brings you closer to a calm, resilient center. Peace isn't about the absence of chaos; it's about finding stillness within it.

Chapter 20: Finding Peace Through Meditation

Getting Clear and Calm from the Inside Out

When I got out of prison, I had one main goal: to heal. After years of strain, I knew I needed something to help me rebuild emotionally, mentally, and physically. Let's keep it real—I didn't know much about meditation when I started, and I wasn't exactly convinced it would do much. But I was willing to try anything to get my life back on track.

The Power of Stillness Life after prison wasn't the same as before. I couldn't just jump back into things; I had to take time to understand what I needed to feel whole again. Meditation was something I tried out of curiosity, but it quickly became more than that. Sitting quietly, even just for a few minutes, gave me a space to breathe and reconnect with myself. It felt like my mind had been racing for years, and finally, I had permission to just let it be.

Here's the deal: stillness isn't just about feeling calm; it's about building a foundation that helps you handle whatever comes next. Meditation gave me that foundation. By finding peace in the quiet moments, I began to feel more grounded, more in control of my emotions. It was like hitting the reset button each day, and slowly but surely, I started to feel the healing take shape.

Meditation and Happiness Meditation didn't just bring calm; it gave me a chance to find real happiness again. After prison, I knew happiness wouldn't come from things or achievements alone; it had to come from within. Meditation helped me uncover that inner peace, even when life was far from perfect. By tuning into myself instead of looking outside for fulfillment, I learned how to cultivate joy that couldn't be shaken by life's ups and downs.

To keep it real, meditation didn't magically fix everything overnight, but it set me on a path to reconnect with happiness. When I sit down to meditate, I'm creating space for gratitude, hope, and a renewed sense of purpose. And these are feelings I still nurture today—meditation isn't a one-and-done thing; it's something I keep coming back to, to help me stay grounded and keep my happiness alive.

Exercise for the Reader: Beginner's Meditation Practice If you're new to meditation, try this simple practice:

1. **Find a quiet space where you can sit comfortably.**
2. **Set a timer for five minutes—you don’t need a lot of time to start feeling the benefits.**
3. **Focus on your breathing, feeling each inhale and exhale. When your mind wanders, gently bring it back to your breath.**

This practice isn’t about clearing your mind completely—it’s about giving yourself a few minutes to just be. Each time you come back to your breath, you’re building resilience and creating room for peace.

CHAPTER 21: TUNING BRAIN FREQUENCIES BOOSTING CONFIDENCE AND COURAGE SUPERCHARGING YOUR MIND TO BOOST CALM, COURAGE, AND CONFIDENCE

When I first started meditating, I had no idea about brain frequencies or how they worked. But as I dug deeper, I learned that the rhythms in our brains actually play a huge role in how we think, feel, and respond to the world. Here's the deal: understanding your brain's frequencies is like unlocking a secret manual that can help you find the states of mind that serve you best—whether that's calm, confidence, or courage.

Discovering Brain Waves After prison, I was searching for ways to build myself back up from the inside out, and that's when I stumbled onto the power of brain waves. Your brain operates at different frequencies depending on your state of mind: • Beta Waves: This is your everyday alert state—good for focus, but too much can mean stress.

- **Alpha Waves**: When you're relaxed but alert, you're in alpha. This frequency supports creativity, calm, and clarity.
- **Theta Waves**: Theta is where deep relaxation, intuition, and creativity happen. It's the state you access in meditation and helps with healing.
- **Delta Waves**: Delta is the slowest frequency, linked to deep sleep and restoration.

To keep it real, understanding these frequencies wasn't some magic fix, but it was a huge step toward understanding how my mind worked and how I could harness different states to find peace, confidence, and strength.

Level Up Confidence and Self-Esteem with Alpha and Theta One of the biggest breakthroughs for me was learning that relaxation and confidence are connected. When I access alpha and theta states in meditation, I find a calm that lets me reconnect with my strengths. In those moments, fear and self-doubt take a backseat, and I can focus on the things that make me feel good about myself. It's not about ignoring the hard stuff, but about creating a space where I can see things clearly and recognize my worth.

When you regularly practice getting into an alpha or theta state, you're training your brain to build self-assurance from within. That confidence becomes part of you, something that doesn't rely on anyone else's approval.

Finding Courage with Theta and Delta Courage doesn't just come from adrenaline; it comes from a deeper place within you. When I access delta waves through deep relaxation or rest, I feel recharged, ready to face whatever comes my way. Theta waves, which often show up in meditation, help me approach challenges with curiosity rather than fear.

These frequencies allow me to tap into a steady, grounded courage that's not about hype or hype but about real strength. Here's what's up: once you know how to reach these states, you're giving yourself the tools to handle life's toughest moments with a clear mind and a strong spirit.

CHAPTER 22: HAPPINESS: YOUR SECRET TO STAYING YOUNG–MIND, BODY AND SPIRIT HAPPINESS: YOUR SECRET TO STAYING YOUNG, MIND, BODY, AND SPIRIT

Let me share something personal and have silently been a bit sensitive about. I was 55 years old when I was sentenced to seven years in prison, and I was 62 when I walked out. Those seven years felt like they were stolen from me, and I wanted them back. I felt a deep determination to redeem that time, pursue every goal and dream I'd had before conviction. I wanted to make up for those years, not just by living, but by thriving.

During those years, I spent a lot of time thinking about age, time, and what it means to grow older. I studied anti-aging and longevity, and what I learned changed the way I see aging itself. I came to understand that, sure, getting older is inevitable—but aging, in a lot of ways, is optional. You don't have to let the years define what you can or can't do. Age can truly just be a number, and happiness is one of the keys to staying young at heart.

Happiness and Staying Young Science backs this up: happiness does more than make you feel good—it actually impacts your health. When you're happy, your body releases chemicals that boost your mood,

support heart health, and even strengthen your immune system. It's like a natural anti-aging formula. On the other hand, stress and unhappiness create wear and tear on the body, making us feel and look older than we are.

Reducing Stress to Live Longer Here's the deal—stress ages us, plain and simple. But finding happiness, those little things that make life enjoyable, can actually dial back the impact of stress. When you focus on what brings you joy, peace, and contentment, you're training your body to be stronger and more resilient. After all I'd been through, I knew I had to let go of bitterness, focus on gratitude, and reconnect with what made me feel alive. Happiness became my secret weapon, redeeming lost time and energy. Grounded in the words of Ephesians 5:14-21 and committed to doing my part for good health, I stay driven toward a life that's not just long but also fulfilling.

It's Never Too Late to Be Happy Whether you're 25, 55, or 75, it's never too late to choose happiness. Many people believe their best years are behind them, but happiness isn't tied to age. It's tied to choice. You can decide, at any age, to pursue the things that make you feel good, whether that's learning something new, taking up a hobby, reconnecting with people, or simply learning to live with more gratitude.

Practical Tips for a Youthful, Happy Life Here are some simple ways to start living with more joy, vitality, and yes, youthfulness: • Daily Joy Check-In: Write down three things each day that made you happy. They don't have to be big—small moments count just as much. This habit will help you focus on the good around you.

- **Stay Connected:** Reach out to people who uplift you. Building relationships and staying socially active is one of the best things you can do to keep yourself young and grounded.
- **Keep Learning:** Try something new, even if it's as small as reading about a topic that interests you. Lifelong learning keeps your mind sharp and your outlook fresh.

- **Let Go of What Weighs You Down:** Holding onto regret, bitterness, or grudges ages us. Practice letting go, whether it's by writing down your feelings and then discarding the paper, or simply choosing to forgive.

Make Happiness Your Fountain of Youth Happiness is a choice you can make every day. It's not just about feeling good in the moment; it's about building a life that keeps you young at heart. You don't have to let your past, or your age, define what's possible. If you take one thing away from this, let it be this: happiness is more than just an emotion; it's a way to live well, keep yourself healthy, and add life to your years. So go ahead—choose to get happy or die trying, and watch how it changes not just your outlook but your whole life.

Reader's Exercise: Your Secret to Staying Young at Heart 1. Daily Joy Journal

Each day for the next week, write down three things that made you smile, laugh, or feel genuinely happy. They don't have to be big moments—simple things like a good cup of coffee, a favorite song, or a nice chat with a friend count, too. This exercise trains you to notice and appreciate everyday happiness, boosting your mood and resilience.

2. Reconnect for Happiness

Think of one person who brings you joy but whom you haven't connected with in a while. Reach out this week for a chat, coffee, or a catch-up call. Social connections strengthen happiness and health, so make it a point to nurture the relationships that add happiness to your life.

3. Try Something New

Pick a small activity you've always wanted to try or learn—a recipe, a new walking route, or even a quick online class. Doing something new keeps your mind active, engages your curiosity, and brings a fresh spark to your day, no matter your age.

4. Let Go and Move On
Think of one regret, worry, or past moment you're ready to release. Write it down, acknowledge it, then crumple up the paper and throw it away. This small action symbolizes letting go and opens up room for new happiness to enter.

These exercises help you cultivate daily joy, connect with others, stay curious, and release the past, giving you more moments of happiness to keep you young at heart.

Acknowledgment

First and foremost, I give credit to the God of the universe, who has guided me through every challenge and blessing. Without His grace, wisdom, and strength, none of this would have been possible. Every lesson, every experience, and every word of this book comes from the journey He set me on, teaching me to rise, to heal, and to find purpose. My hope is that these pages have inspired you to live your life with joy and resilience, pursuing happiness with all your heart, determined to **get happy or die trying**.

BONUS CHAPTER: I'M THE BOSS OF ME

But Not The God Of Me

Let me keep it real—there was a time in prison when I was angry with God. I felt like God had let me down. I thought, "God, you knew I didn't have the intent to commit fraud, so why did you let me get convicted?" Fraud requires intent, and God knew there was no intent. Unexcusable neglect? Sure, I own that. But fraud, no.

During my trial, it felt like everyone who could've defended me "pleaded the Fifth." For a while, I thought God had too. I couldn't understand why God didn't show up to help clear my name. I was hurt, angry, and confused.

But as time passed, I was reminded of a truth I'd heard before: God has a purpose for everything God allows to happen in our lives. That doesn't mean it's easy to see or understand at the moment. I began to shift my thinking from, "Why did this happen to me?" "What's the purpose in this?"

Looking back, I believe part of that purpose was to get me here—to this moment, writing this book, sharing my story, and preparing for whatever comes next. It was about letting go, releasing my need for control, and letting God be God in my life.

Owning My Role, Trusting God's Plan
When I say, "I'm the boss of me, but not the God of me," I mean I take responsibility for my decisions and actions, but I also recognize there's a bigger plan in motion. Being the boss of my life means I step up, make

choices, and own the consequences. But it also means knowing when to step back and let God handle what I can't.

In prison, I had to face this reality. I couldn't undo the conviction or change the outcome. But what I could do was ask God to show me the purpose in it. When I stopped being angry and started being open, I began to see God was still working—even in the middle of the chaos.

Why Do Bad Things Happen?

This is one of the hardest questions: If God is good, why do bad things happen? I wrestled with this question a lot.

Here's what I've come to understand: God gave us free will—the ability to choose good or evil. Unfortunately, some people use that freedom to make harmful choices, and sometimes innocent people get hurt as a result. Living the large life, I made bad choices, resulting in neglect that hurt people financially and otherwise. And it cost me seven years of my life.

But here's what I learned: God can take even the worst situations and turn them into something meaningful. That doesn't mean the pain disappears or that we'll always understand why things happen. It means that with time and trust, we can see how God weaves purpose into our struggles.

Letting Go and Letting God

In prison, I had to let go of my anger, my frustration, and my need to understand everything. I had to get to a place where I could say, "God, I don't get this, but I trust you're still in control."

Letting go doesn't mean giving up. It means trusting God to handle what you can't and focusing on what you can do—growing, healing, and moving forward.

Steps to Let God Be God in Your Life

Be Honest with God:
Don't hide your emotions. If you're angry, confused, or hurt, tell God. Being real with God is the first step toward healing.

Ask the Right Questions:
Shift from asking, "Why did this happen?" to "What can I learn from this? What's the purpose in it?" It's a powerful mindset shift.

Focus on What You Can Control:
You can't always change what happens to you, but you can control how you respond. Ask God for strength and resilience.

Let Go of the Need to Understand Everything:
Some answers may come later, and some you may never get. Trust that God's plan is bigger than what you can see right now.

Lean Into Gratitude:
Even in tough times, find something to be thankful for. Gratitude helps you see where God is still at work in your life.

God Wants You to Be Happy

Here's something many people miss: God wants you to live a happy, fulfilled life. Not the kind of happiness tied to material things or fleeting moments, but deep, lasting joy rooted in peace, love, and purpose.

That doesn't mean life will always be easy or perfect. Challenges will come, but with God, you can face them with confidence and calm. God's version of happiness isn’t about avoiding the hard stuff—it’s about thriving through it.

Final Thoughts

Looking back, I can see that my time in prison wasn't wasted. It was painful, yes, but it became a turning point—a chance to confront my anger, let go of my need for control, and trust God's bigger plan.

When I say, "I'm the boss of me, but not the God of me," it's a reminder that I don't have to figure everything out. God's got the bigger picture. My job is to do my part, own my choices, and trust God with the rest.

God didn't leave me in my hardest moments, and God won't leave you either. When you let go and let God be God, you'll see that even the hardest times have a purpose. Your story isn't over—God's still writing it. Trust the process, keep moving forward, and know that God wants you to live a life full of peace, love, meaning, and happiness.

www.ingramcontent.com/pod-product-compliance
Lightning Source LLC
LaVergne TN
LVHW082251150826
845677LV00009B/1604
* 9 7 9 8 2 3 0 5 0 2 9 2 0 *